ORDER OF COMPLINE

CONTENTS

PREFACE

INTRODUCTION

Truth and reality all come down to the simple fact that "God so loved the world he gave his only Son."[1] This verse is perhaps one of the most well-known verses in all Scripture. That can cause some to brush it off as a known fact. But this isn't just a fact. It is a truth that is meant to melt the deepest parts of the human heart. The most compelling and radical tale of the universe is that the God who made reality pursues you and me, inviting us into an intimate relationship with him through the cross. This relationship sparks a fire in the human heart. Yet, like any fire, the flame must be kindled, and dry wood must be added. This is prayer. Frequent prayer is and must be one of the most foundational parts of the Christian life.

Through the centuries, many devotions and aids have been developed to help the Christian follow Christ's calling to "pray without ceasing."[2] Arguably, the crown jewel of Christian devotion is the Liturgy of the Hours. As the Church grew in the first century, she adopted the Jewish tradition of praying the psalms. This form of prayer slowly developed into what is known today as the Liturgy of the Hours or the Divine Office.

Following Scripture when the psalmist exclaims, "seven times a day I praise you,"[3] the Liturgy of the Hours is broken into seven parts: the Office of Readings, Morning Prayer (Lauds), Mid-Morning Prayer (Terce), Midday Prayer (Sext), Afternoon Prayer (None), Evening Prayer (Vespers), and Night Prayer (Compline). When praying the full Office, one reads through the entire Book of Psalms in a month. The goal is to truly live out God's word hour by hour, constantly returning to this devotion.

In previous centuries, this prayer was limited to religious and clergy. However, today the emphasis has been to include the

---

[1] John 3:16
[2] 1 Thessalonians 5:17
[3] Psalm 119:164

laity in this treasure. As *Sacrosanctum Concilium* states, the Liturgy of the Hours "is the voice of the Church, that is of the whole mystical body publicly praising God."[4] This booklet contains only Compline, the last prayer of the day. It is meant to prepare one's soul for sleep and, if God wills, death.

After the Second Vatican Council, the Church rearranged Compline so that the psalms alternated throughout the week. It is a more simplified version of the version used in previous centuries in order to help priests navigate their busy schedules. However, devotion to more traditional forms of worship remain in use today. Thus, for those so inclined, a modern format for Traditional Compline has been provided below. This format is a mix between the ancient monastic version preserved by various traditional monastic orders and the simplified 1960 edition of the Office of Compline.

For Catholics, written prayer is utilized frequently. However, it must be remembered to pray it with intention and to use it as a door to deeper contemplation. Likewise, it is important to remember by praying devotionals such as this, we echo love songs that have been sent heavenward for two thousand years to Almighty God. It is an honor for the Catholic to be able to sing these praises in union with the Church Militant, as well as the Church Suffering and Church Triumphant. My hope is that you find this booklet to be a simple format to participate in such a splendid form of prayer.

HOW TO PRAY THIS COMPLINE

To provide some clarity, a brief summary of how to follow the more difficult parts of the rubrics are provided here. The first section is titled "Sunday Night Prayer I." This is due to the Catholic calendar which considers Saturday night to be the vigil for Sunday. Thus, Saturday night prayer is "Sunday Night Prayer I" and Sunday night itself is titled "Sunday Night Prayer II."

---

[4] Sacrosanctum Concilium

The italicized are instructions and are not to be said aloud. At the red crosses, the Christian is encouraged to sign themselves with the cross. If one says Compline in a group, the leader says non-bolded words. The people respond with the bold. As for the psalms, traditionally the Liturgy of the Hours is split into two choirs who alternate paragraphs. If in a group, the readers may break into two sections. Group I prays the bold paragraph and Group II prays the non-bolded. Aside from these brief notes, the italicized instructions should guide the reader adequately.

SUNDAY NIGHT PRAYER I

The Pastor or Leader begins

O God, + come to my assistance.
– **Lord, make haste to help me.**
Glory to the Father, and to the Son, and to the Holy Spirit:
– **as it was in the beginning, is now, and will be forever.**
Amen. Alleluia.

The Leader may then say

Let us take a moment to examine our conscience.

Silence may be kept.

Leader and People.

I confess to almighty God
and to you, my brothers and sisters,
that I have greatly sinned,
in my thoughts and in my words,
in what I have done and in what I have failed to do,
(*strike breast*) **through my fault, through my fault, through my**
most grievous fault therefore I ask blessed Mary ever-Virgin,
all the Angels and Saints,
and you, my brothers and sisters,
to pray for me to the Lord our God.

Leader

May almighty God have mercy on us, forgive us of our sins, and
bring us to everlasting life.
– **Amen.**

Kyrie, eleison.   *Lord, have mercy.*
– **Kyrie, eleison.**   ***Lord, have mercy.***

Christe, eleison.   *Christ, have mercy.*
– **Christe, eleison.**   ***Christ, have mercy.***

Kyrie, eleison.   *Lord, have mercy.*
– **Kyrie, eleison.**   ***Lord, have mercy.***

Leader and People sing a hymn together. One option is provided here.

HYMN
All Praise To You, O God, This Night

All praise to You, O God, this night
For all the blessings of the light;
Keep us, we pray, O King of kings,
Beneath Your own almighty wings.
Forgive us, Lord, through Christ your Son,
Whatever wrong this day we've done;
Your peace give to the world, O Lord,
That we might live in one accord.
Enlighten us, O blessed Light,
and give us rest throughout this night.
O strengthen us, that for Your sake,
We all may serve You when we wake.

The Leader says or sings the antiphon.

PSALMODY
Antiphon 1

Have mercy, Lord, and hear my prayer.

The People then alternate in two sections saying each section of the psalm.

Psalm 4   *Cum invocarem*

When I call, answer me, O God of justice;
From anguish you released me;
Have mercy and hear me!

O men, how long will your hearts be closed,
will you love what is futile and seek what is false?

It is the Lord who grants favors to those whom he loves;
The Lord hears me whenever I call him.

Fear him; do not sin; ponder on your bed and be still.
Make justice your sacrifice and trust in the Lord.

"What can bring us happiness?" many say.
Let the light of your face shine on us, O Lord.

You have put into my heart a greater joy
than they have from abundance of corn and new wine.

I will lie down in peace and sleep comes at once
for you alone, Lord, make me dwell in safety.

Glory to the Father, and to the Son, and to the Holy Spirit:
– **as it was in the beginning, is now, and will be forever.**

Amen.

All say Antiphon 1 together.

Have mercy, Lord, and hear my prayer.

Antiphon 2

In the silent hours of the night, bless the Lord.

Psalm 134   *Ecce nunc*

O come, bless the Lord,
All you who serve the Lord
Who stand in the house of the Lord,

In the courts of the house of our God.

Lift up your hands to the holy place
And bless the Lord through the night.

May the Lord bless you from Zion,
He who made both heaven and earth.

Glory to the Father, and to the Son, and to the Holy Spirit:
– as it was in the beginning, is now, and will be forever.

Amen.

All say Antiphon 2 together.

In the silent hours of the night, bless the Lord.

READING

Deuteronomy 6:4-7

Hear, O Israel: The Lord is our God, the Lord alone! Therefore, you shall love the Lord, your God, with all your heart, and with all your soul, and with all your strength. Take to heart these words which I enjoin on you today. Drill them into your children. Speak of them at home and abroad, whether you are busy or at rest.

The reader and the people alternate with the Responsory

RESPONSORY
Into your hands, O Lord, I commend my spirit.
- Into your hands, O Lord, I commend my spirit.

You have redeemed us, Lord God of truth.
- I commend my spirit.

Glory to the Father, and to the Son, and to the Holy Spirit,
- **Into your hands, O Lord, I commend my spirit.**

The leader says the antiphon, then the people join for the canticle

GOSPEL CANTICLE
Antiphon: Protect us Lord, as we stay awake; watch over us as we sleep, that awake, we may keep watch with Christ, and asleep, rest in his peace

Cantincle of Simeon (Luke 2:29-32)

**Lord, + now you let your servant go in peace;
Your word has been fulfilled:**

**My own eyes have seen the salvation
Which you have prepared in the sight of every people:**

**A light to reveal you to the nations
And the glory of your people Israel.**

**Glory be to the Father, and to the Son, and to the Holy Spirit:
as it was in the beginning, is now and will be for ever. Amen**

Antiphon: **Protect us Lord, as we stay awake; watch over us as we sleep, that awake, we may keep watch with Christ, and asleep, rest in his peace.**

FINAL PRAYER

The leader then says

Let us Pray

Be with us throughout this night, when day comes may we rise from sleep to rejoice in the resurrection of your Christ, who lives and reigns for ever and ever. **Amen.**

Or

Visit, we beseech You this dwelling, and drive far from it the snares of the enemy. May Your holy angels dwell herein to preserve in peace. And let your blessing be upon us always. We ask this through Christ our Lord. **Amen.**

BLESSING

May + the all-powerful Lord grant us a restful night and a peaceful death. **Amen.**

Antiphon or song in honor of the Blessed Virgin Mary

Salve, Regina, Mater misericordiæ, vita, dulcedo, et spes nostra, salve. Ad te clamamus exsules filii Hevæ, Ad te suspiramus, gementes et flentes in hac lacrimarum valle. Eia, ergo, advocata nostra, illos tuos misericordes oculos ad nos converte; Et Jesum, benedictum fructum ventris tui, nobis post hoc exsilium ostende. O clemens, O pia, O dulcis Virgo Maria.	**Hail, holy Queen, Mother of mercy, our life, our sweetness and our hope. To thee do we cry, poor banished children of Eve. To thee do we send up our sighs, mourning and weeping in this valley of tears. Turn, then, most gracious advocate, thine eyes of mercy toward us, and after this, our exile, show unto us the blessed fruit of thy womb, Jesus. O clement, O loving, O sweet Virgin Mary.**
Ora pro nobis, sancta Dei	Pray for us, O holy Mother of

Genitrix.
– **Ut digni efficiamur promissionibus Christi.**

Oremus.

Omnipotens sempiterne Deus, qui gloriosæ Virginis Matris Mariæ corpus et animam, ut dignum Filii tui habitaculum effici mereretur, Spiritu Sancto cooperante præparasti: da, ut cuius commemoratione lætamur; eius pia intercessione, ab instantibus malis, et a morte perpetua liberemur. Per eundem Christum Dominum nostrum. **Amen.**

God.
– **That we may be made worthy of the promises of Christ.**

Let us pray

Almighty and everlasting God, Who by the working of the Holy Spirit didst prepare both body and soul of the glorious Virgin Mother, Mary, that she might deserve to be made a worthy dwelling for Thy Son, grant that we who rejoice in her memory, may, by her loving intercession, be delivered from present evils and from lasting death, through the same Christ our Lord. **Amen.**

SUNDAY NIGHT PRAYER II

The Pastor or Leader begins

O God, + come to my assistance.
– **Lord, make haste to help me.**
Glory to the Father, and to the Son, and to the Holy Spirit:
– **as it was in the beginning, is now, and will be forever.**
Amen. Alleluia.

The Leader may then say

Let us take a moment to examine our conscience.

Silence may be kept.

Leader and People.

I confess to almighty God
and to you, my brothers and sisters,
that I have greatly sinned,
in my thoughts and in my words,
in what I have done and in what I have failed to do,
(*strike breast*) **through my fault, through my fault, through my**
most grievous fault therefore I ask blessed Mary ever-Virgin,
all the Angels and Saints,
and you, my brothers and sisters,
to pray for me to the Lord our God.

Leader

May almighty God have mercy on us, forgive us of our sins, and
bring us to everlasting life.
– **Amen.**

Kyrie, eleison.   *Lord, have mercy.*
– **Kyrie, eleison.**   ***Lord, have mercy.***

Christe, eleison.	*Christ, have mercy.*
– **Christe, eleison.**	***Christ, have mercy.***

Kyrie, eleison.	*Lord, have mercy.*
– **Kyrie, eleison.**	***Lord, have mercy.***

Leader and People sing a hymn together. One option is provided here.

HYMN
Te Lucis

Before the ending of the day
Creator of the world we pray
That with thy wonted favor thou
Wouldst be our guard and keeper now

From all ill dreams defend our eyes
From nightly fears and phantasies
Tread under foot our ghostly foe
That no pollution we may know

Oh Father that we ask be done
Through Jesus Christ Thine only Son
Who with the Holy Ghost and Thee
Doth live and reign eternally. Amen.

The Leader says or sings the antiphon.

PSALMODY
Antiphon 1

Night holds no terrors for me sleeping under God's wings.

The People then alternate in two sections saying each section of the psalm.

Psalm 91   Qui habitat

He who dwells in the shelter of the Most High

and abides in the shade of the Almighty
says to the Lord: "My refuge,
my stronghold, my God in whom I trust!"

It is he who will free you from the snare
of the fowler who seeks to destroy you;
he will conceal you with his pinions
and under his wings you will find refuge.

**You will not fear the terror of the night
nor the arrow that flies by day,
nor the plague that prowls in the darkness
nor the scourge that lays waste at noon.**

A thousand may fall at your side,
ten thousand fall at your right,
you, it will never approach;
his faithfulness is buckler and shield.

**Your eyes have only to look
to see how the wicked are repaid,
you who have said: "Lord, my refuge!"
and have made the Most High your dwelling.**

Upon you no evil shall fall,
no plague approach where you dwell.
For you has he commanded his angels,
to keep you in all your ways.

**They shall bear you upon their hands
lest you strike your foot against a stone.
On the lion and the viper you will tread
and trample the young lion and the dragon.**

Since he clings to me in love, I will free him;
protect him for he knows my name.

When he calls I shall answer: "I am with you."
I will save him in distress and give him glory.

**With length of life I will content him;
I shall let him see my saving power.**

Glory to the Father, and to the Son, and to the Holy Spirit:
– **as it was in the beginning, is now, and will be forever.**

Amen.

All say Antiphon 1 together.

Night holds no terrors for me sleeping under God's wings.

A lector or reader is selected to say the following

READING
Revelation 22:4-5

They shall see him face to face and bear his name on their
foreheads. The night shall be no more. They will need no light
from lamps or the sun, for the Lord God shall give them light,
and
they shall reign forever.

The reader and the people alternate with the Responsory

RESPONSORY
Into your hands, O Lord, I commend my spirit.
- **Into your hands, O Lord, I commend my spirit.**

You have redeemed us, Lord God of truth.
- **I commend my spirit.**

Glory to the Father, and to the Son, and to the Holy Spirit,
- **Into your hands, O Lord, I commend my spirit.**

The leader says the antiphon, then the people join for the canticle

GOSPEL CANTICLE

Antiphon: Protect us Lord, as we stay awake; watch over us as we sleep, that awake, we may keep watch with Christ, and asleep, rest in his peace

Cantincle of Simeon (Luke 2:29-32)

**Lord, + now you let your servant go in peace;
your word has been fulfilled:
my own eyes have seen the salvation**

**which you have prepared in the sight of every people:
a light to reveal you to the nations
and the glory of your people Israel.**

**Glory be to the Father, and to the Son, and to the Holy Spirit:
as it was in the beginning, is now and will be for ever. Amen**

Antiphon: **Protect us Lord, as we stay awake; watch over us as we sleep, that awake, we may keep watch with Christ, and asleep, rest in his peace.**

FINAL PRAYER

The leader then says

Let us Pray

Lord, we have celebrated today the mystery of the rising of Christ to new life. May we now rest in peace, safe from all that could harm us, and rise again refreshed and joyful to praise you throughout another day. We ask this through Christ our Lord. **Amen.**

Or

Visit, we beseech You this dwelling, and drive far from it the snares of the enemy. May Your holy angels dwell herein to preserve in peace. And let your blessing be upon us always. We ask this through Christ our Lord. **Amen.**

BLESSING
May + the all-powerful Lord grant us a restful night and a peaceful death. **Amen.**

Antiphon or song in honor of the Blessed Virgin Mary

Regina caeli, laetare, alleluia:
quia quem meruisti portare, alleluia.
Resurrexit, sicut dixit, alleluia.
Ora pro nobis Deum, alleluia.

Queen of Heaven, rejoice, alleluia.
For He whom you did merit to bear, alleluia.
Has risen as he said, alleluia.
Pray for us to God, alleluia.

Gaude et laetare, Virgo Maria, alleluia.
- Quia surrexit Dominus vere, alleluia.

Rejoice and be glad, O Virgin Mary, alleluia.
- For the Lord has truly risen, alleluia.

Oremus

Let us Pray

Deus, qui per resurrectionem Filii tui, Domini nostri Iesu Christi, mundum laetificare dignatus es: praesta, quaesumus; ut per eius Genetricem Virginem Mariam, perpetuae capiamus

O God, who gave joy to the world through the resurrection of Thy Son, our Lord Jesus Christ, grant we beseech Thee, that through the intercession of the Virgin Mary, His Mother, we may

gaudia vitae. Per eundem Christum Dominum nostrum. **Amen.**

obtain the joys of everlasting life. Through the same Christ our Lord. **Amen.**

MONDAY NIGHT PRAYER

The Pastor or Leader begins

O God, + come to my assistance.
– **Lord, make haste to help me.**
Glory to the Father, and to the Son, and to the Holy Spirit:
– **as it was in the beginning, is now, and will be forever.**
Amen. Alleluia.

The Leader may then say

Let us take a moment to examine our conscience.

Silence may be kept.

Leader and People.

I confess to almighty God
and to you, my brothers and sisters,
that I have greatly sinned,
in my thoughts and in my words,
in what I have done and in what I have failed to do,
(*strike breast*) **through my fault, through my fault, through my**
most grievous fault therefore I ask blessed Mary ever-Virgin,
all the Angels and Saints,
and you, my brothers and sisters,
to pray for me to the Lord our God.

Leader

May almighty God have mercy on us, forgive us of our sins, and
bring us to everlasting life.
– **Amen.**

Kyrie, eleison.   *Lord, have mercy.*
– **Kyrie, eleison.**   ***Lord, have mercy.***

Christe, eleison.   *Christ, have mercy.*
– **Christe, eleison.**   ***Christ, have mercy.***

Kyrie, eleison.   *Lord, have mercy.*
– **Kyrie, eleison.**   ***Lord, have mercy.***

Leader and People sing a hymn together. One option is provided here.

HYMN
Creator of the Stars of Night

Creator of the stars of night,
your people's everlasting light,
O Christ, Redeemer of us all,
we pray you, hear us when we call.

In sorrow that the ancient curse
should doom to death a universe,
you came to save a ruined race
with healing gifts of heav'nly grace.

When earth drew on to darkest night,
you came, but not in splendor bright,
not as a king, but the child
of Mary, virgin mother mild.

At your great name, majestic now,
all knees must bend, all hearts must bow;
all things on earth with one accord
join those in heav'n to call you Lord.

To God the Father, God the Son,
and God the Spirit, Three in One,
praise, honor, might, and glory be
from age to age eternally.

The Leader says or sings the antiphon.

PSALMODY
Antiphon 1

O Lord, our God, unwearied is your love for us.

The People then alternate in two sections saying each section of the psalm.

Psalm 86   *Inclina, Domine*

Turn your ear, O Lord, and give answer
for I am poor and needy.
Preserve my life, for I am faithful:
save the servant who trusts in you.

You are my God; have mercy on me, Lord,
for I cry to you all day long.
Give joy to your servant, O Lord,
for to you I lift up my soul.

O Lord, you are good and forgiving,
full of love to all who call.
Give heed, O Lord, to my prayer
and attend to the sound of my voice.

In the day of distress I will call
and surely you will reply.
Among the gods there is none like you, O Lord;
nor work to compare with yours.

All the nations shall come to adore you
and glorify your name, O Lord:
for you are great and do marvelous deeds,
you who alone are God.

Show me, Lord, your way
so that I may walk in your truth.
Guide my heart to fear your name.

I will praise you, Lord my God, with all my heart
and glorify your name for ever;
for your love to me has been great:
you have saved me from the depths of the grave.

The proud have risen against me;
ruthless men seek my life:
to you they pay no heed.

But you, God of mercy and compassion,
slow to anger, O Lord,
abounding in love and truth,
turn and take pity on me.

O give your strength to your servant
and save your handmaid's son.
Show me the sign of your favor
that my foes may see to their shame
that you console me and give me your help.

Glory to the Father, and to the Son, and to the Holy Spirit:
– as it was in the beginning, is now, and will be forever.

Amen.

All say Antiphon 1 together.

O Lord, our God, unwearied is your love for us.

A lector or reader is selected to say the following

READING
Thessalonians 5:9-10

God has destined us for acquiring salvation through our Lord Jesus Christ. He died for us, that all of us, whether awake or asleep, together might live with him.

The reader and the people alternate with the Responsory

RESPONSORY
Into your hands, O Lord, I commend my spirit.
- **Into your hands, O Lord, I commend my spirit.**

You have redeemed us, Lord God of truth.
- **I commend my spirit.**

Glory to the Father, and to the Son, and to the Holy Spirit,
- **Into your hands, O Lord, I commend my spirit.**

The leader says the antiphon, then the people join for the canticle

GOSPEL CANTICLE
Antiphon: Protect us Lord, as we stay awake; watch over us as we sleep, that awake, we may keep watch with Christ, and asleep, rest in his peace

Cantincle of Simeon (Luke 2:29-32)

Lord, + now you let your servant go in peace;
your word has been fulfilled:
my own eyes have seen the salvation

which you have prepared in the sight of every people:
a light to reveal you to the nations
and the glory of your people Israel.

Glory be to the Father, and to the Son, and to the Holy Spirit:
as it was in the beginning, is now and will be for ever. Amen

Antiphon: **Protect us Lord, as we stay awake; watch over us as we sleep, that awake, we may keep watch with Christ, and asleep, rest in his peace.**

FINAL PRAYER

The leader then says

Let us Pray

Lord, give our bodies restful sleep and let the work we have done today bear fruit in eternal life. We ask this through Christ our Lord. **Amen.**

BLESSING

May + the all-powerful Lord grant us a restful night and a peaceful death. Amen.

Antiphon or song in honor of the Blessed Virgin Mary

Ave, María, grátia plena, Dóminus tecum. Benedicta tu in muliéribus, et benedíctus fructus ventris tui, Iesus. Sancta María, Mater Dei, ora pro nobis peccatoribus nunc et in hora mortis nostrae. Amen.	**Hail Mary, full of grace, the Lord is with thee. Blessed art thou amongst women, and blessed is the fruit of thy womb, Jesus. Holy Mary, Mother of God, pray for us sinners, now, and at the hour of our death. Amen.**

TUESDAY NIGHT PRAYER

The Pastor or Leader begins

O God, + come to my assistance.
– **Lord, make haste to help me.**
Glory to the Father, and to the Son, and to the Holy Spirit:
– **as it was in the beginning, is now, and will be forever.
Amen. Alleluia.**

The Leader may then say

Let us take a moment to examine our conscience.

Silence may be kept.

Leader and People.

**I confess to almighty God
and to you, my brothers and sisters,
that I have greatly sinned,
in my thoughts and in my words,
in what I have done and in what I have failed to do,**
(*strike breast*) **through my fault, through my fault, through my
most grievous fault therefore I ask blessed Mary ever-Virgin,
all the Angels and Saints,
and you, my brothers and sisters,
to pray for me to the Lord our God.**

Leader

May almighty God have mercy on us, forgive us of our sins, and
bring us to everlasting life.
– **Amen.**

Kyrie, eleison.   *Lord, have mercy.*
– **Kyrie, eleison.**   ***Lord, have mercy.***

| Christe, eleison. | *Christ, have mercy.* |
| **– Christe, eleison.** | ***Christ, have mercy.*** |

| Kyrie, eleison. | *Lord, have mercy.* |
| **– Kyrie, eleison.** | ***Lord, have mercy.*** |

Leader and People sing a hymn together. One option is provided here.

HYMN
Day is Done but Love Unfailing

Day is done, but love unfailing
Dwells ever here;
Shadows fall, but hope prevailing,
Calms every fear.
Loving Father, none forsaking,
Take our hearts, of Love's own making,
Watch our sleeping, guard our waking,
Be always near.

Dusk descends, but light unending
Shines through our night;
You are with us, ever lending
New strength to sight:
One in love, your truth confessing,
One in hope of heaven's blessing,
May we see, in love's possessing,
Love's endless light!

Eyes will close, but you unsleeping
Watch by our side;
Death may come, in loves safekeeping
Still we abide
God of love, all evil quelling,
Sin forgiving, fear dispelling,
Stay with us, our hearts indwelling,
This eventide.

PSALMODY
Antiphon 1

Do not hide your face from me; in you I put my trust.

The People then alternate in two sections saying each section of the psalm.

Psalm 143:1-11   *Domine, exaudi orationem meam*

Lord, listen to my prayer:
Turn your ear to my appeal.
You are faithful, you are just; give answer.
Do not call your servant to judgment
for no one is just in your sight.

The enemy pursues my soul;
he has crushed my life to the ground;
he has made me dwell in darkness
like the dead, long forgotten.
Therefore my spirit fails;
my heart is numb within me.

I remember the days that are past.
I ponder all your works.
I muse on what your hand has wrought
and to you I stretch out my hands.
Like a parched land my soul thirsts for you.

Lord make haste and answer;
for my spirit fails within me.
Do no hide your face
lest I become like those in the grave.

In the morning let me know your love

for I put my trust in you.
Make me know the way I should walk:
to you I lift up my soul.

Rescue me, Lord, from my enemies;
I have fled to you for refuge.
Teach me to do your will
for you, O Lord, are my God.
Let your good spirit guide me
in ways that are level and smooth.

For your name's sake, Lord, save my life;
in your justice save my soul from distress.

Glory to the Father, and to the Son, and to the Holy Spirit:
– as it was in the beginning, is now, and will be forever.

Amen.

All say Antiphon 1 together.

Do not hide your face from me; in you I put my trust.

READING
1 Peter 5:8-9a

Stay sober and alert. Your opponent the devil is prowling like a roaring lion looking for someone to devour. Resist him, solid in your faith.

The reader and the people alternate with the Responsory

RESPONSORY
Into your hands, O Lord, I commend my spirit.
- Into your hands, O Lord, I commend my spirit.

You have redeemed us, Lord God of truth.

- I commend my spirit.

Glory to the Father, and to the Son, and to the Holy Spirit,
- Into your hands, O Lord, I commend my spirit.

The leader says the antiphon, then the people join for the canticle

GOSPEL CANTICLE
Antiphon: Protect us Lord, as we stay awake; watch over us as we sleep, that awake, we may keep watch with Christ, and asleep, rest in his peace

Cantincle of Simeon (Luke 2:29-32)

Lord, + now you let your servant go in peace;
your word has been fulfilled:
my own eyes have seen the salvation

which you have prepared in the sight of every people:
a light to reveal you to the nations
and the glory of your people Israel.

Glory be to the Father, and to the Son, and to the Holy Spirit:
as it was in the beginning, is now and will be for ever. Amen

Antiphon: **Protect us Lord, as we stay awake; watch over us as we sleep, that awake, we may keep watch with Christ, and asleep, rest in his peace.**

FINAL PRAYER

The leader then says

Let us Pray

Lord, fill this night with your radiance. May we sleep in peace and rise with joy to welcome the light of a new day in your name. We ask this through Christ our Lord. **Amen.**

BLESSING

May + the all-powerful Lord grant us a restful night and a peaceful death. **Amen.**

Antiphon or song in honor of the Blessed Virgin Mary

Ave, María, grátia plena, Dóminus tecum. Benedicta tu in muliéribus, et benedíctus fructus ventris tui, Iesus.
Sancta María, Mater Dei, ora pro nobis peccatoribus nunc et in hora mortis nostrae. Amen.

Hail Mary, full of grace, the Lord is with thee. Blessed art thou amongst women, and blessed is the fruit of thy womb, Jesus.
Holy Mary, Mother of God, pray for us sinners, now, and at the hour of our death. Amen.

WEDNESDAY NIGHT PRAYER

The Pastor or Leader begins

O God, + come to my assistance.
– **Lord, make haste to help me.**
Glory to the Father, and to the Son, and to the Holy Spirit:
– **as it was in the beginning, is now, and will be forever.**
Amen. Alleluia.

The Leader may then say

Let us take a moment to examine our conscience.

Silence may be kept.

Leader and People.

I confess to almighty God
and to you, my brothers and sisters,
that I have greatly sinned,
in my thoughts and in my words,
in what I have done and in what I have failed to do,
(*strike breast*) **through my fault, through my fault, through my**
most grievous fault therefore I ask blessed Mary ever-Virgin,
all the Angels and Saints,
and you, my brothers and sisters,
to pray for me to the Lord our God.

Leader

May almighty God have mercy on us, forgive us of our sins, and
bring us to everlasting life.
– **Amen.**

Kyrie, eleison.   *Lord, have mercy.*
– **Kyrie, eleison.**   *Lord, have mercy.*

Christe, eleison.   *Christ, have mercy.*
– **Christe, eleison.**   ***Christ, have mercy.***

Kyrie, eleison.   *Lord, have mercy.*
– **Kyrie, eleison.**   ***Lord, have mercy.***

Leader and People sing a hymn together. One option is provided here.

HYMN
Let All Mortal Flesh Keep Silence

Let all mortal flesh keep silence,
and with fear and trembling stand;
ponder nothing earthly-minded,
for with blessing in his hand,
Christ our God to earth descendeth,
our full homage to demand.

King of kings, yet born of Mary,
as of old on earth he stood,
Lord of lords, in human vesture,
in the body and the blood,
he will give to all the faithful
his own self for heav'nly food.

Rank on rank the host of heaven
spreads its vanguard on the way,
as the Light of light descendeth
from the realms of endless day,
that the pow'rs of hell may vanish
as the darkness clears away.

At his feet the six-winged seraph,
cherubim, with sleepless eye,
veil their faces to the presence,
as with ceaseless voice they cry,
"Alleluia, alleluia,

alleluia, Lord Most High!"

The Leader says or sings the antiphon.

PSALMODY
Antiphon 1

Lord God, be my refuge and my strength.

The People then alternate in two sections saying each section of the psalm.

Psalm 31:1-6   *In te, Domine*
In you, Lord, I take refuge.
Let me never be put to shame.
In your justice, set me free,
Hear me, and speedily rescue me.

Be a rock of refuge for me.
a mighty stronghold to save me,
for you are my rock, my stronghold.
For your name's sake, lead me and guide me.

Release me from the snares they have hidden
for you are my refuge, Lord.
Into your hands I commend my spirit.
It is you who will redeem me, Lord.

Glory to the Father, and to the Son, and to the Holy Spirit:
– as it was in the beginning, is now, and will be forever.

Amen.

All say Antiphon 1 together.

Lord God, be my refuge and my strength.

Antiphon 2

34

Out of the depths I cry to you, Lord.

Psalm 130   *De profundis*

Out of the depths I cry to you, O Lord,
Lord, hear my voice!
O let your ears be attentive
To the voice of my pleading.

If you, O Lord, should mark our guilt,
Lord, who would survive?
But with you is found forgiveness:
for this we revere you.

My soul is waiting for the Lord,
I count on his word.
My soul is longing for the Lord
More than a watchman for daybreak.
Let the watchman count on daybreak
And Israel on the Lord.

Because with the Lord there is mercy
and the fullness of redemption,
Israel indeed he will redeem
From all its iniquity.

Glory to the Father, and to the Son, and to the Holy Spirit:
– as it was in the beginning, is now, and will be forever.

Amen.

All say Antiphon 2 together.

Out of the depths I cry to you, Lord.

A lector or reader is selected to say the following

READING
Ephesians 4:26-27

If you are angry, let it be without sin. The sun must not go down on your wrath; do not give the devil a chance to work on you.

RESPONSORY
Into your hands, O Lord, I commend my spirit.
- **Into your hands, O Lord, I commend my spirit.**

You have redeemed us, Lord God of truth.
- **I commend my spirit.**

Glory to the Father, and to the Son, and to the Holy Spirit,
- **Into your hands, O Lord, I commend my spirit.**

The leader says the antiphon, then the people join for the canticle

GOSPEL CANTICLE
Antiphon: Protect us Lord, as we stay awake; watch over us as we sleep, that awake, we may keep watch with Christ, and asleep, rest in his peace

Cantincle of Simeon (Luke 2:29-32)
Lord, + now you let your servant go in peace;
your word has been fulfilled:
my own eyes have seen the salvation

which you have prepared in the sight of every people:
a light to reveal you to the nations
and the glory of your people Israel.

Glory be to the Father, and to the Son, and to the Holy Spirit:
as it was in the beginning, is now and will be for ever. Amen

Antiphon: **Protect us Lord, as we stay awake; watch over us as we sleep, that awake, we may keep watch with Christ, and asleep, rest in his peace.**

FINAL PRAYER

The leader than says

Let us Pray

Lord Jesus Christ, you have given your followers an example of gentleness and humility, a task that is easy, a burden that is light. Accept the prayers and work of this day, and give us the rest that will strengthen us to render more faithful service to you who live and reign for ever and ever. **Amen.**

BLESSING

May + the all-powerful Lord grant us a restful night and a peaceful death. **Amen.**

Antiphon or song in honor of the Blessed Virgin Mary

Memorare, O piissima Virgo Maria, non esse auditum a saeculo, quemquam ad tua currentem praesidia, tua implorantem auxilia, tua petentem suffragia, esse derelictum. Ego tali animatus confidentia, ad te, Virgo Virginum, Mater, curro, ad te venio, coram te gemens peccator assisto. Noli, Mater Verbi, verba mea despicere; sed audi

Remember, O most gracious Virgin Mary, that never was it known that anyone who fled to thy protection, implored thy help, or sought thy intercession was left unaided. Inspired with this confidence, I fly to thee, O Virgin of virgins, my Mother; to thee do I come; before thee I stand, sinful and sorrowful. O Mother of the Word Incarnate, despise

propitia et exaudi. Amen.

not my petitions, but in thy mercy hear and answer me. Amen.

THURSDAY NIGHT PRAYER

The Pastor or Leader begins

O God, + come to my assistance.
– **Lord, make haste to help me.**
Glory to the Father, and to the Son, and to the Holy Spirit:
– **as it was in the beginning, is now, and will be forever.**
Amen. Alleluia.

The Leader may then say

Let us take a moment to examine our conscience.

Silence may be kept.

Leader and People.

I confess to almighty God
and to you, my brothers and sisters,
that I have greatly sinned,
in my thoughts and in my words,
in what I have done and in what I have failed to do,
(*strike breast***) through my fault, through my fault, through my**
most grievous fault therefore I ask blessed Mary ever-Virgin,
all the Angels and Saints,
and you, my brothers and sisters,
to pray for me to the Lord our God.

Leader

May almighty God have mercy on us, forgive us of our sins, and
bring us to everlasting life.
– **Amen.**

Kyrie, eleison.   *Lord, have mercy.*
– **Kyrie, eleison.**   ***Lord, have mercy.***

Christe, eleison.   *Christ, have mercy.*
– **Christe, eleison.**   ***Christ, have mercy.***

Kyrie, eleison.   *Lord, have mercy.*
– **Kyrie, eleison.**   ***Lord, have mercy.***

Leader and People sing a hymn together. One option is provided here.

HYMN
Holy God We Praise Thy Name

Holy God, we praise thy name.
God of all, we bow before thee.
All on earth your scepter claim;
all in heav'n above adore thee.
Infinite thy vast domain,
everlasting is thy reign.

Hark, the loud celestial hymn,
angel choirs above are raising.
Cherubim and seraphim,
in unceasing chorus praising,
fill the heav'ns with sweet accord:
Holy, holy, holy Lord.

Lo! the apostolic train
join thy sacred name to hallow.
Prophets swell the glad refrain,
and the blessed martyrs follow,
and, from morn till set of sun,
through the church the song goes on.

Holy Author, Holy Word,
Holy Spirit, three we name thee;
still, one holy voice is heard:
undivided God, we claim thee,

**and adoring bend the knee,
while we own the mystery.**

The Leader says or sings the antiphon.

PSALMODY
Antiphon 1

In you, my God, my body will rest in hope.

The People then alternate in two sections saying each section of the psalm.

Psalm 16   Conserva me

Preserve me, God, I take refuge in you.
I say to the Lord: "You are my God.
My happiness lies in you alone."

**He has put into my heart a marvelous love
for the faithful ones who dwell in his land.
Those who choose other gods increase their sorrows.
Never will I offer their offerings of blood.
Never will I take their name upon my lips.**

O Lord, it is you who are my portion and cup;
it is you yourself who are my prize.
The lot marked out for me is my delight:
welcome indeed the heritage that falls to me!

**I will bless the Lord who gives me counsel,
who even at night directs my heart.
I keep the Lord ever in my sight:
since he is at my right hand, I shall stand firm.**

And so my heart rejoices, my soul is glad;
even my body shall rest in safety.
For you will not leave my soul among the dead,

nor let your beloved know decay.

You will show me the path of life,
the fullness of joy in your presence,
at your right hand happiness forever.

Glory to the Father, and to the Son, and to the Holy Spirit:
– **as it was in the beginning, is now, and will be forever.**

Amen.

All say Antiphon 1 together.

In you, my God, my body will rest in hope.

A lector or reader is selected to say the following

READING
1 Thessalonians 5:23

May the God of peace make you perfect in holiness. May he
preserve you whole and entire, spirit, soul, and body,
irreproachable at the coming of our Lord Jesus Christ.

The reader and the people alternate with the Responsory

RESPONSORY
Into your hands, O Lord, I commend my spirit.
- **Into your hands, O Lord, I commend my spirit.**

You have redeemed us, Lord God of truth.
- **I commend my spirit.**

Glory to the Father, and to the Son, and to the Holy Spirit,
- **Into your hands, O Lord, I commend my spirit.**

The leader says the antiphon, then the people join for the canticle

GOSPEL CANTICLE

Antiphon: Protect us Lord, as we stay awake; watch over us as we sleep, that awake, we may keep watch with Christ, and asleep, rest in his peace

Cantincle of Simeon (Luke 2:29-32)

Lord, + now you let your servant go in peace;
your word has been fulfilled:
my own eyes have seen the salvation

which you have prepared in the sight of every people:
a light to reveal you to the nations
and the glory of your people Israel.

Glory be to the Father, and to the Son, and to the Holy Spirit:
as it was in the beginning, is now and will be for ever. Amen

Antiphon: **Protect us Lord, as we stay awake; watch over us as we sleep, that awake, we may keep watch with Christ, and asleep, rest in his peace.**

FINAL PRAYER

The leader then says

Let us Pray

Lord God, send peaceful sleep to refresh our tired bodies. May your help always renew us and keep us strong in your service. We ask this through Christ our Lord. **Amen.**

BLESSING

May + the all-powerful Lord grant us a restful night and a peaceful death. **Amen.**

Antiphon or song in honor of the Blessed Virgin Mary

Alma Redemptoris Mater, quæ pervia cæli porta manes, et stella maris, succurre cadenti, surgere qui curat, populo: tu quæ genuisti, natura mirante, tuum sanctum Genitorem Virgo prius ac posterius, Gabrielis ab ore sumens illud Ave, peccatorum miserere. Amen.

Lovin mother of the Redeemer, gate of heaven, star of the sea, assist your people who have fallen yet strive to rise again. To the wonderment of nature you bore your Creator, yet remained a virgin after as before. You who received Gabriel's joyful greeting, have pity on us poor sinners. Amen.

FRIDAY NIGHT PRAYER

The Pastor or Leader begins

O God, + come to my assistance.
– **Lord, make haste to help me.**
Glory to the Father, and to the Son, and to the Holy Spirit:
– **as it was in the beginning, is now, and will be forever.**
Amen. Alleluia.

The Leader may then say

Let us take a moment to examine our conscience.

Silence may be kept.

Leader and People.

I confess to almighty God
and to you, my brothers and sisters,
that I have greatly sinned,
in my thoughts and in my words,
in what I have done and in what I have failed to do,
(*strike breast*) **through my fault, through my fault, through my**
most grievous fault therefore I ask blessed Mary ever-Virgin,
all the Angels and Saints,
and you, my brothers and sisters,
to pray for me to the Lord our God.

Leader

May almighty God have mercy on us, forgive us of our sins, and
bring us to everlasting life.
– **Amen.**

Kyrie, eleison.   *Lord, have mercy.*
– **Kyrie, eleison.**   ***Lord, have mercy.***

Christe, eleison.	*Christ, have mercy.*
– **Christe, eleison.**	***Christ, have mercy.***

Kyrie, eleison.	*Lord, have mercy.*
– **Kyrie, eleison.**	***Lord, have mercy.***

Leader and People sing a hymn together. One option is provided here.

HYMN
Christe, Qui, Splendor Et Dies

**Christ, thou who art the light and day,
who chasest nightly shades away,
thyself the Light of Light confessed,
and promiser of radiance blest:**

**O holy Lord, we pray to thee,
throughout the night our guardian be;
in thee vouchsafe us to repose,
all peaceful till the night shall close.**

**O let our eyes due slumber take,
our hearts to thee forever wake:
and let thy right hand from above
shield us who turn to thee in love.**

**O strong defender, hear our prayers,
repel our foes and break their snares,
and govern thou thy servants here,
those ransomed with thy life-blood dear.**

**Almighty Father, this accord
through Jesus Christ, thy Son our Lord,
Who with the Holy Ghost and thee
doth reign through all eternity. Amen.**

The Leader says or sings the antiphon.

PSALMODY
Antiphon 1

Day and night I cry to you, my God.

The People then alternate in two sections saying each section of the psalm.

Psalm 88   *Domine, Deus salutis meæ*

Lord my God, I call for help by day;
I cry at night before you.
Let my prayer come into your presence.
O turn your ear to my cry.

For my soul is filled with evils;
my life is on the brink of the grave.
I am reckoned as one in the tomb:
I have reached the end of my strength.

like those among the dead;
like the slain lying in their graves;
like those you remember no more,
cut off, as they are, from your hand.

You have laid me in the depths of the tomb,
in places that are dark, in the depths.
Your anger weighs down upon me:
I am drowned beneath your waves.

You have taken away my friends
and made me hateful in their sight.
Imprisoned, I cannot escape;
my eyes are sunken with grief.

I call to you, Lord, all the day long;
to you I stretch out my hands.
Will you work your wonders for the dead?

Will the shades stand and praise you?

Will your love be told in the grave
or your faithfulness among the dead?
Will your wonders be known in the dark
or your justice in the land of oblivion?

As for me, Lord, I call to you for help:
in the morning my prayer comes before you.
Lord, why do you reject me?
Why do you hide your face?

Wretched, close to death from my youth,
I have borne your trials; I am numb.
Your fury has swept down upon me;
your terrors have utterly destroyed me.

They surround me all the day like a flood,
they assail me all together.
Friend and neighbor you have taken away:
my one companion is darkness.

Glory to the Father, and to the Son, and to the Holy Spirit:
– as it was in the beginning, is now, and will be forever.

Amen.

All say Antiphon 1 together.

Day and night I cry to you, my God.

A lector or reader is selected to say the following

READING
Jeremiah 14:9a

You are in our midst, O Lord, your name we bear: do not forsake us, O Lord, our God!

The reader and the people alternate with the Responsory

RESPONSORY
Into your hands, O Lord, I commend my spirit.
- **Into your hands, O Lord, I commend my spirit.**

You have redeemed us, Lord God of truth.
- **I commend my spirit.**

Glory to the Father, and to the Son, and to the Holy Spirit,
- **Into your hands, O Lord, I commend my spirit.**

The leader says the antiphon, then the people join for the canticle

GOSPEL CANTICLE
Antiphon: Protect us Lord, as we stay awake; watch over us as we sleep, that awake, we may keep watch with Christ, and asleep, rest in his peace

Cantincle of Simeon (Luke 2:29-32)

Lord, + now you let your servant go in peace;
your word has been fulfilled:
my own eyes have seen the salvation

which you have prepared in the sight of every people:
a light to reveal you to the nations
and the glory of your people Israel.

Glory be to the Father, and to the Son, and to the Holy Spirit:
as it was in the beginning, is now and will be for ever. Amen

Antiphon: **Protect us Lord, as we stay awake; watch over us as we sleep, that awake, we may keep watch with Christ, and asleep, rest in his peace.**

FINAL PRAYER

The leader then says

Let us Pray

All-powerful God, keep us united with your Son in his death and burial so that we may rise to new life with him, who lives and reigns for ever and ever. **Amen.**

BLESSING

May + the all-powerful Lord grant us a restful night and a peaceful death. **Amen.**

Antiphon or song in honor of the Blessed Virgin Mary

Salve, Regina, Mater misericordiæ, vita, dulcedo, et spes nostra, salve. Ad te clamamus exsules filii Hevæ, Ad te suspiramus, gementes et flentes in hac lacrimarum valle. Eia, ergo, advocata nostra, illos tuos misericordes oculos ad nos converte; Et Jesum, benedictum fructum ventris tui, nobis post hoc exsilium ostende. O clemens, O pia, O dulcis Virgo Maria.

Hail, holy Queen, Mother of mercy, our life, our sweetness and our hope. To thee do we cry, poor banished children of Eve. To thee do we send up our sighs, mourning and weeping in this valley of tears. Turn, then, most gracious advocate, thine eyes of mercy toward us, and after this, our exile, show unto us the blessed fruit of thy womb, Jesus. O clement, O loving, O sweet Virgin Mary.

Ora pro nobis, sancta Dei Genitrix.

– **Ut digni efficiamur promissionibus Christi.**

Oremus.

Omnipotens sempiterne Deus, qui gloriosæ Virginis Matris Mariæ corpus et animam, ut dignum Filii tui habitaculum effici mereretur, Spiritu Sancto cooperante præparasti: da, ut cuius commemoratione lætamur; eius pia intercessione, ab instantibus malis, et a morte perpetua liberemur. Per eundem Christum Dominum nostrum. **Amen.**

Pray for us, O holy Mother of God.

– **That we may be made worthy of the promises of Christ.**

Let us pray

Almighty and everlasting God, Who by the working of the Holy Spirit didst prepare both body and soul of the glorious Virgin Mother, Mary, that she might deserve to be made a worthy dwelling for Thy Son, grant that we who rejoice in her memory, may, by her loving intercession, be delivered from present evils and from lasting death, through the same Christ our Lord. **Amen.**

TRADITIONAL COMPLINE

INCIPIT
The Pastor or Leader begins

Iube, Dómine, benedícere.
– **Noctem quiétam et finem perféctum concédat nobis Dóminus omnípotens. Amen.**

LECTIO
1 Petrus 5:8-9

Fratres: Sóbrii estóte, et vigiláte: quia adversárius vester diábolus tamquam leo rúgiens círcuit, quærens quem dévoret: cui resístite fortes in fide.

The leader then says,

Tu autem, Dómine, miserére nobis.
– **Deo grátias.**

Adiutórium nóstrum + in nómine Dómini.
– **Qui fecit cælum et terram.**

A brief pause follows to examine the heart. Or, the Pater Noster is said silently.

[Pater noster, qui es in cælis, sanctificétur nomen tuum: advéniat regnum tuum: fiat volúntas tua, sicut in cælo et in

START
The Pastor or Leader begins

Grant, Lord, a blessing.
– **May almighty God grant us a quiet night and a perfect end. Amen.**

READING
1 Peter 5:8-9

Brothers: Be sober and watch: because your adversary the devil, as a roaring lion, goeth about seeking whom he may devour. Whom resist ye, strong in faith.

The leader then says,

But thou, O Lord, have mercy upon us.
– **Thanks be to God.**

Our help is + in the name of the Lord.
– **Who made heaven and earth.**

A brief pause follows to examine the heart. Or, the Our Father is said silently.

[Our Father, who art in heaven, hallowed be thy name. Thy kingdom come. Thy will be done one earth as it is in heaven. Give

terra. Panem nostrum cotidiánum da nobis hódie: et dimítte nobis débita nostra, sicut et nos dimíttimus debitóribus nostris: et ne nos indúcas in tentatiónem: sed líbera nos a malo. Amen.]

The leader and the people pray aloud,

Confíteor Deo omnipoténti, beátæ Maríæ semper Vírgini, beáto Michaéli Archángelo, beáto Ioánni Baptístæ, sanctis Apóstolis Petro et Paulo, et ómnibus Sanctis, quia peccávi nimis, cogitatióne, verbo et ópere: *(percutit sibi pectus)* **mea culpa, mea culpa, mea máxima culpa. Ídeo precor beátam Maríam semper Vírginem, beátum Michaélem Archángelum, beátum Ioánnem Baptístam, sanctos Apóstolos Petrum et Paulum, et omnes Sanctos, oráre pro me ad Dóminum Deum nostrum.**

The leader or priest then says,

Misereátur nostri omnípotens Deus, et dimíssis peccátis nostris, perdúcat nos ad vitam ætérnam. **Amen.**
Indulgéntiam, + absolutiónem et remissiónem peccatórum nostrórum tríbuat nobis

---

us this day our daily bread. And forgive us our trespasses, as we forgive those who trespass against us. And lead us not into temptation: But deliver us from evil. Amen.]

The leader and the people pray aloud,

I confess to almighty God, to blessed Mary ever Virgin, to blessed Michael the Archangel, to blessed John the Baptist, to the holy Apostles Peter and Paul, and to all the Saints, that I have sinned exceedingly in thought, word and deed: *(strike breast)* **through my fault, through my fault, through my most grievous fault. Therefore I beseech blessed Mary ever Virgin, blessed Michael the Archangel, blessed John the Baptist, the holy Apostles Peter and Paul, and all the Saints, to pray for me to the Lord our God.**

The leader or priest then says,

May almighty God have mercy on us, forgive us our sins, and bring us to everlasting life. **Amen.**
May the almighty + and merciful Lord grant us pardon, absolution and remission of our sins. **Amen.**

omnípotens et miséricors Dóminus. **Amen.**

Convérte nos *(signum crucis super cor tuum)* Deus, salutáris noster.
– **Et avérte iram tuam a nobis.**

Deus + in adiutórium meum inténde.
– **Dómine, ad adiuvándum me festína.**

Glória Patri, et Fílio, et Spirítui Sancto.
– **Sicut erat in princípio, et nunc, et semper, et in sǽcula sæculórum. Amen. Allelúia.**

The Leader says or sings the antiphon.

PSALMI
Antiphona 1

Miserere, Domine, et exaudi orationem meam.

The People then alternate in two sections saying each section of the psalm.

Psalmus 4   Cum invocarem

Cum invocárem exaudívit me Deus iustítiæ meæ: in tribulatióne dilatásti mihi. Miserére mei, et exáudi

Turn us then, *(make a cross on your heart)* O God, our savior.
– **And let thy anger cease from us.**
O God, + come to my assistance.

– **Lord, make haste to help me.**

Glory be to the Father, and to the Son, and to the Holy Ghost:
– **as it was in the beginning, is now, and ever shall be, world without end. Amen. Alleluia.**

The Leader says or sings the antiphon.

PSALMODY
Antiphon 1

Have mercy, Lord, and hear my prayer.

The People then alternate in two sections saying each section of the psalm.

Psalm 4   Cum invocarem

**When I called upon him, the God of my justice heard me: when I was in distress, thou hast enlarged me.
Have mercy on me: and hear**

54

oratiónem meam.

my prayer.

Fílii hóminum, úsquequo gravi corde? ut quid dilígitis vanitátem, et quǽritis mendácium?

O ye sons of men, how long will you be dull of heart? Why do you love vanity, and seek after lying?

Et scitóte quóniam mirificávit Dóminus sanctum suum: Dóminus exáudiet me cum clamávero ad eum.

Know ye also that the Lord hath made his holy one wonderful: the Lord will hear me when I shall cry unto him.

Irascímini, et nolíte peccáre: quæ dícitis in córdibus vestris, in cubílibus vestris compungímini.

Be ye angry, and sin not: the things you say in your hearts, be sorry for them upon your beds.

Sacrificáte sacrifícium iustítiæ, et speráte in Dómino. Multi dicunt: Quis osténdit nobis bona?

Offer up the sacrifice of justice, and trust in the Lord: many say, Who sheweth us good things?

Signátum est super nos lumen vultus tui, Dómine: dedísti lætítiam in corde meo.
A fructu fruménti, vini, et ólei sui multiplicáti sunt.

The light of thy countenance, O Lord, is signed upon us: thou hast given gladness in my heart. By the fruit of their corn, their wine, and oil, they are multiplied.

**In pace in idípsum dórmiam, et requiéscam;
Quóniam tu, Dómine, singuláriter in spe constituísti me.**

**In peace in the selfsame I will sleep, and I will rest:
For thou, O Lord, singularly hast settled me in hope.**

Glória Patri, et Fílio, et Spirítui Sancto.
– Sicut erat in princípio, et nunc, et semper, et in sǽcula

Glory be to the Father, and to the Son, and to the Holy Ghost:
– as it was in the beginning, is now, and ever shall be, world

sæculórum. Amen.

Psalmus 90   *Qui habitat*

Qui hábitat in adiutório
Altíssimi, in protectióne Dei cæli
commorábitur.
Dicet Dómino: Suscéptor meus
es tu, et refúgium meum: Deus
meus sperábo in eum.

**Quóniam ipse liberávit me de
láqueo venántium, et a verbo
áspero.**
**Scápulis suis obumbrábit tibi:
et sub pennis eius sperábis.**

Scuto circúmdabit te véritas eius:
non timébis a timóre noctúrno,
A sagítta volánte in die, a negótio
perambulánte in ténebris: ab
incúrsu, et dæmónio meridiáno.

**Cadent a látere tuo mille, et
decem míllia a dextris tuis: ad
te autem non appropinquábit.**
**Verúmtamen óculis tuis
considerábis: et retributiónem
peccatórum vidébis.**

Quóniam tu es, Dómine, spes
mea: Altíssimum posuísti

without end. Amen.

Psalm 90   *Qui habitat*

He that dwelleth in the aid of the
most High, shall abide under the
protection of the God of Jacob.
He shall say to the Lord: Thou
art my protector, and my refuge:
my God, in him will I trust.

**For he hath delivered me from
the snare of the hunters: and
from the sharp word.**
**He will overshadow thee with
his shoulders: and under his
wings thou shalt trust.**

His truth shall compass thee with
a shield: thou shalt not be afraid
of the terror of the night.
Of the arrow that flieth in the
day, of the business that walketh
about in the dark: of invasion, or
of the noonday devil.

**A thousand shall fall at thy
side, and ten thousand at thy
right hand: but it shall not
come nigh thee.**
**But thou shalt consider with
thy eyes: and shalt see the
reward of the wicked.**

Because thou, O Lord, art my
hope: thou hast made the most

refúgium tuum.
Non accédet ad te malum: et
flagéllum non appropinquábit
tabernáculo tuo.

**Quóniam Ángelis suis
mandávit de te: ut custódiant
te in ómnibus viis tuis.
In mánibus portábunt te: ne
forte offéndas ad lápidem
pedem tuum.**

Super áspidem, et basilíscum
ambulábis: et conculcábis
leónem et dracónem.
Quóniam in me sperávit, liberábo
eum: prótegam eum, quóniam
cognóvit nomen meum.

**Clamábit ad me, et ego
exáudiam eum: cum ipso sum
in tribulatióne: erípiam eum et
glorificábo eum.
Longitúdine diérum replébo
eum: et osténdam illi salutáre
meum.**

Glória Patri, et Fílio, et Spirítui
Sancto.
**– Sicut erat in princípio, et
nunc, et semper, et in sǽcula
sæculórum. Amen.**

High thy refuge.
There shall no evil come to thee:
nor shall the scourge come near
thy dwelling.

**For he hath given his angels
charge over thee; to keep thee
in all thy ways.
In their hands they shall bear
thee up: lest thou dash thy foot
against a stone.**

Thou shalt walk upon the asp and
the basilisk: and thou shalt
trample under foot the lion and
the dragon.
Because he hoped in me I will
deliver him: I will protect him
because he hath known my name.

**He shall cry to me, and I will
hear him: I am with him in
tribulation, I will deliver him,
and I will glorify him.
I will fill him with length of
days; and I will shew him my
salvation.**

Glory be to the Father, and to the
Son, and to the Holy Ghost:
**– as it was in the beginning, is
now, and ever shall be, world
without end. Amen.**

Psalmus 134   *Ecce nunc*

Ecce nunc benedícite Dóminum, omnes servi Dómini:
Qui statis in domo Dómini, in átriis domus Dei nostri.

In nóctibus extóllite manus vestras in sancta, et benedícite Dóminum.

Benedícat te Dóminus ex Sion, qui fecit cælum et terram.

Glória Patri, et Fílio, et Spirítui Sancto.
– Sicut erat in princípio, et nunc, et semper, et in sǽcula sæculórum. Amen.

All say Antiphon 1 together.

Miserere, Domine, et exaudi orationem meam.

Leader and People sing this hymn together

HYMNUS
Te Lucis

Te lucis ante términum,
Rerum Creátor, póscimus,
Ut sólita cleméntia
Sis præsul ad custódiam.

Psalm 134   *Ecce nunc*

Behold now bless ye the Lord, all ye servants of the Lord: Who stand in the house of the Lord, in the courts of the house of our God.

In the nights lift up your hands to the holy places, and bless ye the Lord.

May the Lord out of Sion bless thee, he that made heaven and earth.

Glory be to the Father, and to the Son, and to the Holy Ghost:
– as it was in the beginning, is now, and ever shall be, world without end. Amen.

All say Antiphon 1 together.

Have mercy, Lord, and hear my prayer.

Leader and People sing this hymn together

HYMN
Te Lucis

Before the ending of the day
Creator of the world we pray
That with thy wonted favor
thou

58

Procul recédant sómnia,
Et nóctium phantásmata;
Hostémque nóstrum cómprime,
Ne polluántur córpora.

Wouldst be our guard and
keeper now

From all ill dreams defend our
eyes
From nightly fears and
phantasies
Tread under foot our ghostly
foe
That no pollution we may
know

Praesta, Pater piissime,
Patrique compar Unice,
cum Spiritu Paraclito
regnans per omne saeculum.
Amen.

Oh Father that we ask be done
Through Jesus Christ Thine
only Son
Who with the Holy Ghost and
Thee
Doth live and reign eternally.
Amen.

A lector or reader is selected to say the following

A lector or reader is selected to say the following

LECTIO
Ieremias 14:9

READING
Jeremiah 14:9

Tu autem in nobis es, Dómine, et nomen sanctum tuum invocátum est super nos: ne derelínquas nos, Dómine, Deus noster.
– **Deo grátias.**

But thou, O Lord, art among us, and thy name is called upon by us: forsake us not, O Lord our God.
– **Thanks be to God.**

The reader and the people alternate with the Responsory

The reader and the people alternate with the Responsory

RESPONSORIUM
 In manus tuas, Dómine,

RESPONSORY
Into thy hands, O Lord, I

Comméndo spíritum meum.
– **In manus tuas, Dómine,**
Comméndo spíritum meum.
Redemísti nos, Dómine, Deus
veritátis.
– **Comméndo spíritum meum.**
Glória Patri, et Fílio, et Spirítui
Sancto.
– **In manus tuas, Dómine,**
Comméndo spíritum meum.

Custódi nos, Dómine, ut
pupíllam óculi.
– **Sub umbra alárum tuárum**
prótege nos.

Antiphon: Salva nos, Dómine,
vigilántes, custódi nos
dormiéntes; ut vigilémus cum
Christo, et requiescámus in pace.

*Canticum Simeonis (Luc 2:29-
32)*

Nunc dimíttis + servum tuum,
Dómine, secúndum verbum
tuum in pace:

Quia vidérunt óculi mei
salutáre tuum,
Quod parásti ante fáciem
ómnium populórum,

Lumen ad revelatiónem
géntium, et glóriam plebis tuæ

commend my spirit.
– **Into thy hands, O Lord, I**
commend my spirit.
For thou hast redeemed us, O
Lord, God of truth.
– **I commend my spirit.**
Glory be to the Father, and to the
Son, and to the Holy Ghost.
– **Into thy hands, O Lord, do I**
commend my spirit.

Keep us, Lord, as the apple of
thine eye.
– **Protect us under the shadow**
of thy wings.

Antiphon: Protect us, Lord, while
we are awake and safeguard us
while we sleep; that we may keep
watch with Christ, and rest in
peace.
*Cantincle of Simeon (Luke 2:29-
32)*

Now thou dost dismiss thy
servant, O Lord, + according to
thy word in peace;

Because my eyes have seen thy
salvation,
Which thou hast prepared
before the face of all peoples:

A light to the revelation of the
Gentiles, and the glory of thy

Israël.

Glória Patri, et Fílio, et Spirítui Sancto.
Sicut erat in princípio, et nunc, et semper, et in sǽcula sæculórum. Amen.

Antiphon: **Salva nos, Dómine, vigilántes, custódi nos dormiéntes; ut vigilémus cum Christo, et requiescámus in pace.**

The leader then says,

Kyrie, eleison.
Christe, eleison.
Kyrie, eleison.

The Pater Noster is said silently until "and lead us not into temptation,"

Pater noster, [qui es in cælis, sanctificétur nomen tuum: advéniat regnum tuum: fiat volúntas tua, sicut in cælo et in terra. Panem nostrum cotidiánum da nobis hódie: et dimítte nobis débita nostra, sicut et nos dimíttimus debitóribus nostris.] Et ne nos indúcas in tentatiónem – **sed líbera nos a malo. Amen.**

Dómine, exáudi oratiónem meam.

people Israel.

Glory be to the Father, and to the Son, and to the Holy Ghost: as it was in the beginning, is now, and ever shall be, world without end. Amen.

Antiphon: **Protect us, Lord, while we are awake and safeguard us while we sleep; that we may keep watch with Christ, and rest in peace.**

The leader then says,

Lord have mercy on us.
Christ have mercy on us.
Lord have mercy on us.

The Our Father is said silently until "and lead us not into temptation,"

Our Father, [who art in heaven, hallowed be thy name. Thy kingdom come. Thy will be done one earth as it is in heaven. Give us this day our daily bread. And forgive us our trespasses, as we forgive those who trespass against us.]
And lead us not into temptation – **But deliver us from evil. Amen.**

O Lord, hear my prayer.
– **And let my cry come unto**

– **Et clamor meus ad te véniat.**

thee.

ULTIMA ORATIO

The leader then says

Oremus

Vísita, quæsumus, Dómine, habitatiónem istam, et omnes insídias inimíci ab ea lónge repélle: Ángeli tui sancti hábitent in ea, qui nos in pace custódiant; et benedíctio tua sit super nos semper. Per Dóminum nostrum Iesum Christum, Fílium tuum: qui tecum vivit et regnat in unitáte Spíritus Sancti, Deus, per ómnia sǽcula sæculórum. **Amen.**

BENEDICTIO
Dómine, exáudi oratiónem meam.
– **Et clamor meus ad te véniat.**

Benedicámus Dómino.
– **Deo grátias.**
Benedícat et custódiat nos omnípotens et miséricors Dóminus, + Pater, et Fílius, et Spíritus Sanctus. **Amen.**

Antiphona seu cantus in honorem B. M. V.

Salve, Regina, Mater

FINAL PRAYER

The leader then says

Let us Pray

Visit, we beseech thee, O Lord, this dwelling, and drive far from it the snares of the enemy; let thy holy angels dwell herein to preserve us in peace, and let thy blessing be always upon us.Through Jesus Christ, thy Son our Lord, Who liveth and reigneth with thee, in the unity of the Holy Ghost, God, world without end. **Amen.**

BLESSING
O Lord, hear my prayer.

– **And let my cry come unto thee.**
Let us bless the Lord.
– **Thanks be to God.**
The almighty and merciful Lord, + the Father, the Son, and the Holy Ghost, bless us and keep us. **Amen.**

Antiphon or song in honor of the Blessed Virgin Mary

Hail, holy Queen, Mother of mercy, our life, our sweetness

misericordiæ, vita, dulcedo, et spes nostra, salve.
Ad te clamamus exsules filii Hevæ, Ad te suspiramus, gementes et flentes in hac lacrimarum valle.
Eia, ergo, advocata nostra, illos tuos misericordes oculos ad nos converte;
Et Jesum, benedictum fructum ventris tui, nobis post hoc exsilium ostende.
O clemens, O pia, O dulcis Virgo Maria.

Ora pro nobis, sancta Dei Genitrix.
– **Ut digni efficiamur promissionibus Christi.**

Oremus,

Omnipotens sempiterne Deus, qui gloriosæ Virginis Matris Mariæ corpus et animam, ut dignum Filii tui habitaculum effici mereretur, Spiritu Sancto cooperante præparasti: da, ut cuius commemoratione lætamur; eius pia intercessione, ab instantibus malis, et a morte perpetua liberemur. Per eundem Christum Dominum nostrum. **Amen.**

and our hope. **To thee do we cry, poor banished children of Eve. To thee do we send up our sighs, mourning and weeping in this valley of tears. Turn, then, most gracious advocate, thine eyes of mercy toward us, and after this, our exile, show unto us the blessed fruit of thy womb, Jesus. O clement, O loving, O sweet Virgin Mary.**

Pray for us, O holy Mother of God.
– **That we may be made worthy of the promises of Christ.**

Let us pray,

Almighty and everlasting God, Who by the working of the Holy Spirit didst prepare both body and soul of the glorious Virgin Mother, Mary, that she might deserve to be made a worthy dwelling for Thy Son, grant that we who rejoice in her memory, may, by her loving intercession, be delivered from present evils and from lasting death, through the same Christ our Lord. **Amen.**

COLLECTS

INTRODUCTION

What follows below are various Collects of the Church. The word means a collection of all the prayers of the people. Below are thirteen prayers which appeal to the personal life, nine for God and His Church, eleven for the family and neighbors, two for the Eucharist, and five which are substitutes for the prayer at the end of night prayer if the reader wishes. In total the reader is supplied with forty prayers in the Church's rich tradition to aid in deeper contemplative and meditative prayer.

PERSONAL COLLECTS

For Faith, Hope and Love,
Almighty and everlasting God, increase in us the gifts of faith, hope, and charity; and, that we may obtain what you promise, make us love what you command; through Jesus Christ our Lord, who lives and reigns with you and the Holy Spirit, one God, for ever and ever. **Amen.**

For Guidance,
O God, by whom the meek are guided in judgment, and light rises up in darkness for the godly: Grant us, in all our doubts and uncertainties, the grace to ask what you would have us to do, that the Spirit of wisdom may save us from all false choices, and that in your light we may see light, and in your straight path may not stumble; through Jesus Christ our Lord. **Amen.**

For Grace,
Almighty and everlasting God, you are always more ready to hear than we are to pray, and to give more than we either desire or deserve: Pour upon us the abundance of your mercy, forgiving us those things of which our conscience is afraid, and giving us those good things for which we are not worthy to ask, except through the merits and mediation of Jesus Christ our Savior; who

lives and reigns with you and the Holy Spirit, one God, for ever
and ever. **Amen.**

For Mercy,
O God, the protector of all who trust in you, without whom
nothing is strong, nothing is holy: Increase and multiply upon us
your mercy; that, with you as our ruler and guide, we may so
pass through things temporal, that we lose not the things eternal;
through Jesus Christ our Lord, who lives and reigns with you and
the Holy Spirit, one God, for ever and ever. **Amen.**

For Perseverance,
Almighty and merciful God, it is only by your gift that your
faithful people offer you true and laudable service: Grant that we
may run without stumbling to obtain your heavenly promises;
through Jesus Christ our Lord, who lives and reigns with you and
the Holy Spirit, one God, now and for ever. **Amen.**

For Strength,
O God, the strength of all who put their trust in you: Mercifully
accept our prayers; and because in our weakness we can do
nothing good without you, give us the help of your grace, that in
keeping your commandments we may please you both in will
and deed; through Jesus Christ our Lord, who lives and reigns
with you and the Holy Spirit, one God, for ever and ever. **Amen.**

For Growth,
Father, you cut down the unfruitful branch for burning and prune
the fertile to make it bear more fruit. Make us grow like laden
olive trees in your domain, firmly rooted in the power and mercy
of your Son, so that you may gather from us fruit worthy of
eternal life. **Amen.**

For purity,
Almighty God, to whom all hearts are open, all desires known,
and from whom no secrets are hidden: cleanse the thoughts of
our hearts by the inspiration of your Holy Spirit, that we may

love you completely, and rightly magnify your holy name; through Christ our Lord. **Amen.**

For True Repentance,
Almighty and everlasting God, you hate nothing you have made and forgive the sins of all who are penitent: Create and make in us a new and contrite heart, that worthily lamenting our sins and acknowledging our wretchedness, we may obtain of you, the God of all mercy, perfect remission and forgiveness; through Jesus Christ our Lord, who lives and reigns with you and the Holy Spirit, one God, for ever and ever. **Amen.**

For Freedom from Sin,
Set us free, O God, from the bondage of our sins, and give us the liberty of that abundant life which you have made known to us in your Son the Savior Jesus Christ; who lives and reigns with you, in the unity of the Holy Spirit, one God, now and for ever. **Amen.**

When in trouble,
Despise not your people, O almighty God, when they cry out in their affliction, but graciously help them in their tribulation, for the glory of Thy name. Through our Lord Jesus Christ your son, who lives and reigns with Thee, in the unity of the Holy Spirit. **Amen.**

For good weather,
Graciously hear us, O Lord, when we call upon Thee, and grant unto our supplications a calm atmosphere, that we, who are justly afflicted for our sins, may, by Thy protecting mercy, experience pardon. Through our Lord Jesus Christ your son, who lives and reigns with Thee, in the unity of the Holy Spirit. **Amen.**

For friends and those dear to us,
O God, who by the grace of the Holy Spirit hast poured the gifts of charity into the hearts of Thy faithful, grant unto Thy servants and handmaids, for whom we implore Thy merciful love, health

of soul and body, that they may love Thee with all their might and with their whole love may execute what things are pleasing to Thee. Through our Lord Jesus Christ your son, who lives and reigns with Thee, in the unity of the Holy Spirit. **Amen.**

COLLECTS FOR GOD AND THE CHURCH

Of the Holy Trinity,
Almighty God, you have revealed to your Church your eternal Being of glorious majesty and perfect love as one God in Trinity of Persons: Give us grace to continue steadfast in the confession of this faith, and constant in our worship of you, Father, Son, and Holy Spirit; for you live and reign, one God, now and for ever. **Amen.**

To Trust in Jesus,
Almighty God, you have given your only Son to be for us a sacrifice for sin, and also an example of godly life: Give us grace to receive thankfully the fruits of this redeeming work, and to follow daily in the blessed steps of his most holy life; through Jesus Christ your Son our Lord, who lives and reigns with you and the Holy Spirit, one God, now and for ever. **Amen.**

Of the Holy Spirit,
Almighty and most merciful God, grant that by the indwelling of your Holy Spirit we may be enlightened and strengthened for your service; through Jesus Christ our Lord, who lives and reigns with you, in the unity of the Holy Spirit, one God, now and for ever. **Amen.**

For the Church,
Gracious Father, we pray for your holy Catholic Church. Fill it with all truth, in all truth with all peace. Where it is corrupt, purify it; where it is in error, direct it; where in any thing it is amiss, reform it. Where it is right, strengthen it; where it is in want, provide for it; where it is divided, reunite it; for the sake of Jesus Christ your Son our Savior. **Amen.**

For the Unity of the Church,
Almighty Father, whose blessed Son before his passion prayed
for his disciples that they might be one, as you and he are one:
Grant that your Church, being bound together in love and
obedience to you, may be united in one body by the one Spirit,
that the world may believe in him whom you have sent, your Son
Jesus Christ our Lord; who lives and reigns with you, in the unity
of the Holy Spirit, one God, now and for ever. **Amen.**

For all Christians in their vocation,
Almighty and everlasting God, by whose Spirit the whole body
of your faithful people is governed and sanctified: Receive our
supplications and prayers, which we offer before you for all
members of you holy Church, that in their vocation and ministry
they may truly and devoutly serve you; through the Lord and
Savior Jesus Christ, who lives and reigns with you, in the unity
of the Holy Spirit, one God, now and for ever. **Amen.**

For the Diocese,
O God, by your grace you have called us in this Diocese to a
goodly fellowship of faith. Bless our Bishops(s) _____ [and
_____], and other clergy, and all the people. Grant that your
Word may be truly preached and truly heard, your Sacraments
faithfully administered and faithfully received. By your Spirit,
fashion our lives according to the example of your Son, and grant
that we may show the power of your love to all among whom we
live; through Jesus Christ our Lord. **Amen.**

For the Parish,
Almighty and everliving God, ruler of all things in heaven and
earth, hear our prayers for this parish family. Strengthen the
faithful, arouse the careless, and restore the penitent. Grant us all
things necessary for our common life, and bring us all to be of
one heart and mind within your holy Church; through Jesus
Christ our Lord. **Amen.**

For reading the Sacred Scriptures,

Blessed Lord, who caused all holy Scriptures to be written for our learning: Grant us so to hear them, read, mark, learn, and inwardly digest them, that we may embrace and ever hold fast the blessed hope of everlasting life, which you have given us in our Savior Jesus Christ; who lives and reigns with you and the Holy Spirit, one God, for ever and ever. **Amen.**

COLLECTS FOR FAMILY AND NEIGHBORS

For Families,

Almighty God, our heavenly Father, who sets the solitary in families: we commend to your continual care the homes in which your people dwell. Put far from them every root of bitterness, the desire of vainglory, and the pride of life. Fill them with faith, virtue, knowledge, temperance, patience, godliness. Knit together in constant affection those who, in holy wedlock, have been made one flesh. Turn the hearts of the parents to the children, and the hearts of the children to the parents; and so enkindle fervent charity among us all, that we may evermore be kindly affectioned one to another; through Jesus Christ our Lord. **Amen.**

For a husband and wife,

Almighty God, giver of life and love, bless _____ and _____. Grant them wisdom and devotion in the ordering of their common life, that each may be to the other a strength in need, a counselor in perplexity, a comfort in sorrow, and a companion in joy. And so knit their wills together in your will and their spirits in your Spirit, that they may live together in love and peace all the days of their life; through Jesus Christ our Lord. **Amen.**

For the Care of Children,

Almighty God, heavenly Father, you have blessed us with the joy and care of children: Give us calm strength and patient wisdom as we bring them up, that we may teach them to love whatever is just and true and good, following the example of our Savior Jesus Christ. **Amen.**

For the Aged,
Look with mercy, O God our Father, on all whose increasing years bring them weakness, distress, or isolation. Provide for them homes of dignity and peace; give them understanding helpers, and the willingness to accept help; and, as their strength diminishes, increase their faith and their assurance of your love. This we ask in the name of Jesus Christ the Lord. **Amen.**

For Young Person,
God our Father, you see your children growing up in an unsteady and confusing world: Show them that your ways give more life than the ways of the world, and that following you is better than chasing after selfish goals. Help them to take failure, not as a measure of their worth, but as a chance for a new start. Give them strength to hold their faith in you, and to keep alive their joy in your creation; through Jesus Christ our Lord. **Amen.**

For Those Who Live Alone,
Almighty God, whose Son had nowhere to lay his head: Grant that those who live alone may not be lonely in their solitude, but that, following in his steps, they may find fulfillment in loving you and their neighbors; through Jesus Christ our Lord. **Amen.**

For Those We Love,
Almighty God, we entrust all who are dear to us to your never-failing care and love, for this life and the life to come, knowing that you are doing for them better things than we can desire or pray for; through Jesus Christ our Lord. **Amen.**

For Our Enemies,
O God, the Father of all, whose Son commanded us to love our enemies: Lead them and us from prejudice to truth: deliver them and us from hatred, cruelty, and revenge; and in your good time enable us all to stand reconciled before you, through Jesus Christ our Lord. **Amen.**

For the Poor and the Neglected,

Almighty and most merciful God, we remember before you all poor and neglected persons whom it would be easy for us to forget: the homeless and the destitute, the old and the sick, and all who have none to care for them. Help us to heal those who are broken in body or spirit, and to turn their sorrow into joy. Grant this, Father, for the love of your Son, who for our sake became poor, Jesus Christ our Lord. **Amen.**

For the Oppressed,

Look with pity, O heavenly Father, upon the people in this land who live with injustice, terror, disease, and death as their constant companions. Have mercy upon us. Help us to eliminate our cruelty to these our neighbors. Strengthen those who spend their lives establishing equal protection of the law and equal opportunities for all. And grant that every one of us may enjoy a fair portion of the riches of this land; through Jesus Christ our Lord. **Amen.**

For the Victims of Addiction,

O blessed Lord, you ministered to all who came to you: Look with compassion upon all who through addiction have lost their health and freedom. Restore to them the assurance of your unfailing mercy; remove from them the fears that beset them; strengthen them in the work of their recovery; and to those who care for them, give patient understanding and persevering love. **Amen.**

PRAYERS FOR THE EUCHARIST

Before Receiving Communion,

Almighty Father, whose dear Son, on the night before he suffered, instituted the Sacrament of his Body and Blood: Mercifully grant that we may receive it thankfully in remembrance of Jesus Christ the Lord, who in these holy mysteries gives us a pledge of eternal life; and who now lives and reigns with you and the Holy Spirit, one God, for ever and ever. **Amen.**

After Receiving Communion,
O Lord Jesus Christ, who in a wonderful Sacrament has left to us a memorial of your passion: Grant us so to venerate the sacred mysteries of your Body and Blood, that we may ever perceive within ourselves the fruit of your redemption; who lives and reigns with the Father and the Holy Spirit, one God, for ever and ever. **Amen.**

ALTERNATIVE COMPLINE PRAYERS

For defence,
Lighten our darkness, O Lord, and in your great mercy defend us from all perils and dangers of this night; for the love of your only Son, our Savior Jesus Christ. **Amen.**

Be with us always,
Be present, O merciful God, and protect us through the hours of this night, so that we who are wearied by the changes and chances of this life may rest in your eternal changelessness; through Jesus Christ our Lord. **Amen.**

Watch over us,
Look down, O Lord, from your heavenly throne, and illumine this night with your celestial brightness; that by night as by day your people may glorify your holy Name; through Jesus Christ our Lord. **Amen.**

Sustain us,
O God, your unfailing providence sustains the world we live in and the life we live: Watch over those, both night and day, who work while others sleep, and grant that we may never forget that our common life depends upon each other's toil; through Jesus Christ our Lord. **Amen.**

Guard us,

Keep watch, dear Lord, with those who work, or watch, or weep this night, and give your angels charge over those who sleep. Tend the sick, Lord Christ; give rest to the weary, bless the dying, soothe the suffering, pity the afflicted, shield the joyous; and all for your love's sake. **Amen.**

ADORATION AND BENEDICTION

The priest enters with a cope and the Host is incensed as the chant below is sung.

The priest enters with a cope and the Host is incensed as the chant below is sung.

O Salutaris Hostia
Quae caeli pandis ostium.
Bella premunt hostilia;
Da robur, fer auxilium.

O Saving Victim opening wide. The gate of heaven to all below. Our foes press on from every side; Thine aid supply, Thy strength bestow.

Uni trinoque Domino
Sit sempiterna gloria:
Qui vitam sine termino,
Nobis donet in patria.
Amen.

To Thy great name be endless praise. Immortal Godhead, One in Three; Oh, grant us endless length of days, in our true native land with Thee.
Amen.

Adoration of the Blessed Sacrament follows. After a time of silence or various prayers, the priest incenses the Host again as the following is chanted,

Adoration of the Blessed Sacrament follows. After a time of silence or various prayers, the priest incenses the Host again as the following is chanted,

Tantum ergo Sacramentum
Veneremur cernui:
Et antiquum documentum
Novo cedat ritui:
Praestet fides
supplementum
Sensuum defectui.

Down in adoration falling,
Lo! the sacred Host we hail,
Lo! oe'r ancient forms departing
Newer rites of grace prevail;
Faith for all defects supplying,
Where the feeble senses fail.

Genitori, Genitoque
Laus et iubilatio,
Salus, honor, virtus quoque
Sit et benedictio:
Procedenti ab utroque
Compar sit laudatio.Amen.

To the everlasting Father,
And the Son Who reigns on high
With the Holy Spirit proceeding
Forth from each eternally,
Be salvation, honor blessing,
Might and endless majesty.
Amen.

The priest and the people make the following exchange,

Panem de caelo praestitisti eis. (Alleluia)
– **Omne delectamentum in se habentem. (Alleluia)**

Thou hast given them bread from heaven (Alleluia).
– **Having within it all sweetness (Alleluia).**

Oremus

Let us pray

Deus, qui nobis sub sacramento mirabili, passionis tuae memoriam reliquisti: tribue, quaesumus, ita nos corporis et sanguinis tui sacra mysteria venerari, ut redemptionis tuae fructum in nobis iugiter sentiamus. Qui vivis et regnas in saecula saeculorum. **Amen.**

O God, who in this wonderful Sacrament left us a memorial of Thy Passion: grant, we implore Thee, that we may so venerate the sacred mysteries of Thy Body and Blood, as always to be conscious of the fruit of Thy Redemption. Thou who livest and reignest forever and ever. **Amen.**

DIVINAS LAUDES
The people are blessed by the Blessed Sacrament. Then, when He is placed back in the tabernacle, all say the following together in English.

THE DIVINE PRAISES
The people are blessed by the Blessed Sacrament. Then, when He is placed back in the tabernacle, all say the following together in English.

Blessed be God.
Blessed be his holy Name.
Blessed be Jesus Christ, true God and true Man.
Blessed be the name of Jesus.
Blessed be his most Sacred Heart.
Blessed be his most Precious Blood.
Blessed be Jesus in the most holy Sacrament of the altar.
Blessed be the Holy Spirit, the Paraclete.
Blessed be the great Mother of God, Mary most holy.
Blessed be her holy and Immaculate Conception.
Blessed be her glorious Assumption.
Blessed be the name of Mary, Virgin and Mother.
Blessed be Saint Joseph, her most chaste spouse.
Blessed be God in his angels and in his saints.

FINIS

As the priest and servers process out, it is common to sing the following in English,

Holy God, we praise thy name.
God of all, we bow before thee.
All on earth your scepter

Blessed be God.
Blessed be his holy Name.
Blessed be Jesus Christ, true God and true Man.
Blessed be the name of Jesus.
Blessed be his most Sacred Heart.
Blessed be his most Precious Blood.
Blessed be Jesus in the most holy Sacrament of the altar.
Blessed be the Holy Spirit, the Paraclete.
Blessed be the great Mother of God, Mary most holy.
Blessed be her holy and Immaculate Conception.
Blessed be her glorious Assumption.
Blessed be the name of Mary, Virgin and Mother.
Blessed be Saint Joseph, her most chaste spouse.
Blessed be God in his angels and in his saints.

CONCLUSION

As the priest and servers process out, it is common to sing the following in English,

Holy God, we praise thy name.
God of all, we bow before thee.
All on earth your scepter

claim;
all in heav'n above adore
thee.
Infinite thy vast domain,
everlasting is thy reign.

Hark, the loud celestial
hymn,
angel choirs above are
raising.
Cherubim and seraphim,
in unceasing chorus
praising,
fill the heav'ns with sweet
accord:
Holy, holy, holy Lord.

Lo! the apostolic train
join thy sacred name to
hallow.
Prophets swell the glad
refrain,
and the blessed martyrs
follow,
and, from morn till set of
sun,
through the church the song
goes on.

Holy Author, Holy Word,
Holy Spirit, three we name
thee;
still, one holy voice is heard:
undivided God, we claim
thee,
and adoring bend the knee,

claim;
all in heav'n above adore
thee.
Infinite thy vast domain,
everlasting is thy reign.

Hark, the loud celestial
hymn,
angel choirs above are
raising.
Cherubim and seraphim,
in unceasing chorus
praising,
fill the heav'ns with sweet
accord:
Holy, holy, holy Lord.

Lo! the apostolic train
join thy sacred name to
hallow.
Prophets swell the glad
refrain,
and the blessed martyrs
follow,
and, from morn till set of
sun,
through the church the song
goes on.

Holy Author, Holy Word,
Holy Spirit, three we name
thee;
still, one holy voice is heard:
undivided God, we claim
thee,
and adoring bend the knee,

while we own the mystery. | while we own the mystery.

ACKNOWLEDGMENTS

"A Comprehensive Index of Hymns and
Hymnals." *Hymnary.Org*, hymnary.org/. Accessed 31 May
2023.

Christian Prayer: The Liturgy of the Hours. Catholic Book Pub.
Co., 1976.

"Collects and Prayers for All Occasions." *Liturgies.Net*,
www.liturgies.net/Prayers/Collects.htm. Accessed 21 June
2023.

"Divinum Officium," www.divinumofficium.com. Accessed 31
May 2023.

Hoever, Hugo H., and Richard Kugelman. *Saint Joseph
Everyday Missal*. Catholic Book Publishing Co., 1957.

"Index / Contents." *A Collection of Prayers*, 3 Mar. 2022,
acollectionofprayers.com/index-contents/.

Martin, Michael. "Thesaurus Precum Latinarum." *Preces Latinae*, www.preces-latinae.org/preces.html. Accessed 21 June 2023.

O'Brian, Patrick. *Saint Mary, My Everyday Missal and Heritage.* Benziger Brothers, Inc., 1948.

Paul VI. "Sacrosanctum Concilium." *Vatican.Va*, www.vatican.va/archive/hist_councils/ii_vatican_council/documents/vat-ii_const_19631204_sacrosanctum-concilium_en.html. Accessed 31 May 2023.

"USCCB." *Books of the Bible*, bible.usccb.org/bible. Accessed 31 May 2023.

Printed in Great Britain
by Amazon